Imagine a House

A Journey to Fascinating Houses Around the World

Angela Gustafson

Out of the Box
Minneapolis, Minnesota

**Dedicated to
Brian
and the kids of
Bánica, Dominican Republic**

Published by

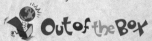

P.O. Box 24234
Minneapolis, MN 55424
www.ootbooks.com

Text: ©2003 Angela Gustafson

World Map: ©2003 Matt Kania

Illustrations: ©2003 Amy Learn, MCAD DesignWorks:
Inside front cover, p. 31, inside back cover; Matthew Mills,
MCAD DesignWorks: p. 6, 7, 8, 10, 12, 14, 16, 18, 20, 22,
24, 26, 28, inside back cover, back cover.

Photographs: ©Angela Gustafson: p. 2; ©Jan Reynolds:
p. 11; ©Nik Wheeler: p. 14, 15, 17, 22, 25; ©Richard
Nowitz: front cover and title page (top left), p. 12, 13,
26; ©Sean Sprague: p. 29; ©Stephen Trimble: p. 8, 24;
©Victor Englebert: front cover and title page (top right,
bottom left and right), p. 9, 10, 16, 18, 19, 20, 21, 23, 27,
28, back cover.

Book design and production: David Farr, ImageSmythe,
St. Paul, Minnesota.

The main text of this book is set in Kandal.

Printed in Minnesota, USA.

Library of Congress Cataloging-in-Publication Data

Gustafson, Angela, 1969-
    Imagine a house : a journey to fascinating houses around the world /by Angela Gustafson.
        p. cm.
Summary: Presents a look at some of the most unusual houses around the world.
    ISBN 0-9726849-0-5
    1. Dwellings—Juvenile literature. 2. Ethnology—Juvenile literature.
    3. Manners and customs—Juvenile literature. [1. Dwellings. 2.
Ethnology. 3. Manners and customs.] I. Title.
    GT172 .G87 2003
    392.3'6—dc21   2002155017

HOW THIS BOOK CAME ABOUT...

Houses burst with color. Dominoes smack on tables. Merengue plays loudly. Smiles stretch wide. Baseballs crack against bats. Bugs creep and crawl. Chickens roam freely. Rice and beans delight. Skin sweats...really sweats. While serving as Peace Corps volunteers in the Dominican Republic, my husband and I were filled with sights and sounds, and tastes and feels...far too many to mention. Some felt close to home and others a world away.

In our community, just a stone's throw from Haiti, we began gathering information on world cultures and creating fun ways to share what we found. For most of the kids, these activities became a first time "trip" out of their home villages. Back home in Minnesota, it didn't seem right to put aside a good thing. So welcome to the first in a unique series of books designed for readers of all ages. Travel the world through vivid photography, enjoy its beauty and learn something along the way!

Houses, with their broad appeal, became topic #1. Well-known photographers submitted hundreds of images from all over the world. Houses come big and small, domed and square, on water and on mountains, one color or multi-colored, made with sticks and made with bricks, and all in between. Even mud houses, estimated to be "home" for half the world's population, stand out in endless varieties. The 12 houses featured in this book do not represent all houses in their respective countries, just as your house would not represent all houses in your country. Rather, they were chosen by groups of kids and adults for the special stories they tell.

Thank you to the people of Bánica, Dominican Republic for the initial inspiration. Thank you to the creative team for giving this book life. Thank you Brian – my best friend and biggest fan. Thank you to our little guys: Zach, Wyatt and Trey... Dream big! And thank **YOU** for picking up this book.

See lots. Do lots,

Angela

Brian and me in front of our "watermelon" house,
Bánica, Dominican Republic—1995

Please...share your thoughts on *Imagine a House* and cast your vote for future topics! E-mail me at: angela@ootbooks.com or write to Out of the Box, P.O. Box 19435, Minneapolis, MN 55419.

Close your eyes.

Imagine a house.

What do you see?

Sleeping under a goat skin tent?

Crawling through a tunnel of snow?

Painting pictures on outside walls?

CANADA

NORTH PACIFIC OCEAN

UNITED STATES

NORTH AMERICA

NORTH ATLANTIC OCEAN

PERU

BRAZIL

SOUTH AMERICA

SOUTH PACIFIC OCEAN

Eating dinner in a beehive?

Floating on an island of grass?

Hopping on a boat to cross the street?

Climbing a ladder to the front door?

ARCTIC OCEAN

EUROPE

ASIA

NORTH PACIFIC OCEAN

ISRAEL
SYRIA
IRAQ
EGYPT
NIGER
ERITREA
SUDAN
AFRICA
KENYA
TANZANIA

PHILIPPINES

INDONESIA

INDIAN OCEAN

AUSTRALIA

SOUTH ATLANTIC OCEAN

ANTARCTICA

All over the world, especially in cities, you can see T-shirts and jeans, fast food chains, streets full of cars, places to shop, shiny new buildings and big fancy houses. But most of the world isn't so modern. Away from the bustle, where tradition runs deep, families build houses with simple materials yet amazing results! Turn the pages and see for yourself.

Adobe Houses

Americas and Northern Africa

Heavy clay soil dug out from the earth is shaped into bricks and baked in the sun. Walls are stacked thick, but rarely too high. Roofs are laid flat and beams often jut. Temperatures blaze up into the hundreds and air conditioning is not part of the plan. Yet all that is needed to keep comfort inside is a smooth coat of mud and prayers for no rain.

Replastering one of America's oldest housing structures
still lived in today—Taos Pueblo, New Mexico

Hundreds of years ago, Native Americans built pueblos (towns) that rose as high as five stories. People entered their pueblos by climbing ladders up to the roofs. Once inside, they climbed more ladders poking through holes in the ceilings. When attackers approached, ladders were pulled up! It wasn't until more peaceful times that doors and windows were added.

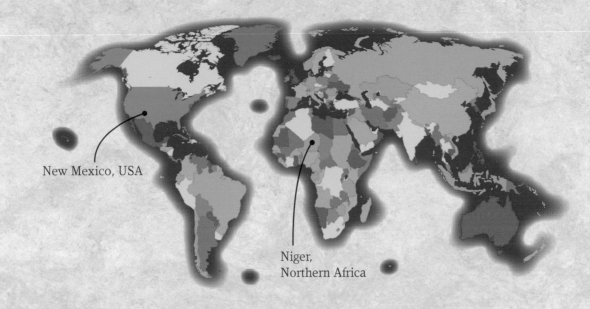

New Mexico, USA

Niger,
Northern Africa

Strolling down main street, off to the market—Tahoua, Niger

Adobe houses are built in hot, dry regions where there is little stone or wood. Daytime temperatures reach as high as 122°F (50°C), and drop as low as 32°F (0°C) at night. The thicker the walls, the cooler the house. The lower the house, the stronger the walls. Many towns have their own special recipe for adobe. Whether roots are added here or gravel is added there, the recipe is usually kept secret from towns down the road.

Igloos

Snow—Arctic Regions
Salt—Eritrea, Africa

Blocks of snow, not too hard and not too soft, cut two feet by four feet, are shaped into a dome. Look up, look down. Look right, look left. No trees, no dirt...just a whole lot of white. Crawl through the tunnel, up into the igloo. The warmer air stays and coldest flows out. Leave your coat on and sit by the fire in this house of snow walls and ice windowpanes.

Igloos come in different flavors: snow, stone, dirt, wood and even salt—Karum Salt Lake, Eritrea

Igloo (from the Inuit word meaning "house") is used to describe domed houses of different materials. The Danakil salt miners above build salt igloos using the only material available to them: salt blocks. These igloos are covered with mats woven from rare clumps of grass. They are built for sleeping and hiding from the sun.

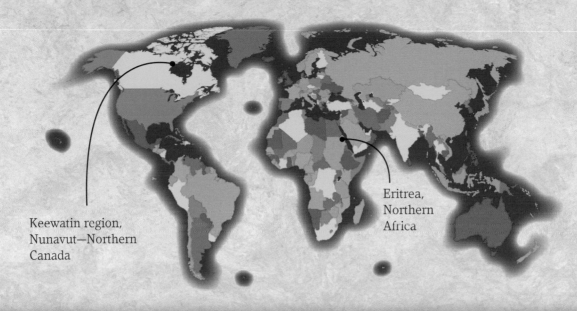

Keewatin region,
Nunavut—Northern
Canada

Eritrea,
Northern
Africa

A father teaching his daughter the Inuit tradition of igloo-building
—west coast of Hudson Bay, northern Canada

The Inuit people (Eskimos) live in the coldest regions of Alaska, Canada, Greenland and
Russia. While most live in permanent wood houses, they continue to build igloos on hunting
trips. The Inuit here are traditionally caribou hunters. The women chew the cleaned
caribou hides to soften them. Then they sew the hides into coats, mittens and boots.

Beehive Houses

Syria

For a very long time, some 8,000 years, beehives have been lived in by more than just bees. People cram stones over humps in the earth. They scoop out the dirt and stand up inside. Mud and straw plaster is caked on the outside, leaving slits here and there for the sun to shine through. When the winter snow flies, beehives stay warm. When the summer sun sizzles, beehives stay cool.

Did you notice the front door? It is a source of pride for many in the countryside—northern Syria

This beehive has a more modern style with wood scaffolds, making cracks in the dome easier to fix. Most people living in Syria are Arabs. An Arab proverb says, "A narrow place can contain a thousand friends." [Meaning: People who love each other can fit into tight places.]

Syria,
The Middle East

A colorful bunch on the family farm—northern Syria

Northern Syria is mostly quiet countryside, with rolling limestone hills.
Kaftans (traditional male gowns) are in fashion alongside jeans and T-shirts.
Women and girls wear their hair long; men and boys wear their hair short.

Reed Houses

Iraq

Channels of water wind through thick marshes in the south of a land known more for its desert. Reeds grow all over, reaching twenty feet high. They are pressed into islands and used to build houses. Thick and thin bundles come together as the frame. Hand-woven mats go up to form walls. Activity abounds outside the front door, from steering boats to catching fish and hunting wild boar.

Father and son hanging out on their island—southern Iraq

Imagine grass growing two basketball hoops high! These tall reeds make tall houses, built by climbing tall stepladders. Even the stepladders are made out of reeds.

Iraq,
The Middle East

Hauling reeds through winding waterways—
Hawr al-Hammar Lake, southern Iraq

Boats also come in handy to visit a friend or catch freshwater fish.
Overhead, ducks and geese fly. Sometimes a stork makes its nest on these
houses. It is thought to bring luck to those living inside.

Houseboats

Most common in Southeast Asia

When land is too costly or crowded to enjoy, people near water can live on their boats. Houseboats may drift or stay parked in one spot. Some are quite cramped while others are roomy. Surrounded by water, some people fish. Others provide tours, cut hair, or cook meals. A few work on land and just sleep on the water. But most spend their lives rarely touching the ground.

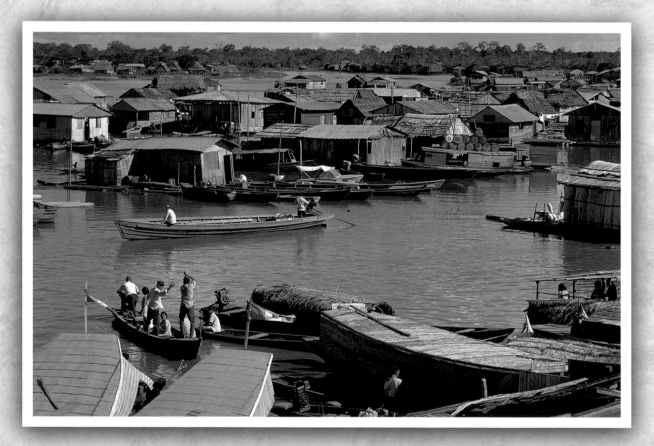

An entire community afloat on the Ucayali River—Pucallpa, Peru

The houseboats here move up and down with the river, depending on rainfall, but typically stay parked in one spot. This busy waterway stemming from the Amazon River is full of activity. Jobs range from running tiny businesses on the water to loading and unloading the many boats passing by.

Philippines,
Southeast Asia

Peru, South America

The Samal boat people live life in tight quarters—Mindanao, Philippines

Except to buy needed items or escape rough weather, most of life is spent
drifting inches from the water. Supports off the sides help keep the boats
from tipping. Canopies over the top provide shade from the sun. People
sleep on mats at night and roll them to the side during the day.

Houses on Stilts

Most common in Southeast Asia

Where buckets of water gush from the sky, the land below can flood in a hurry. Roads become rivers and boats become cars. What once was a porch may soon be a dock. Houses are built out of wood or bamboo. But the key is to sit on a strong set of legs. Play in your tree house with dry ground below. Relax on your island when surrounded by water.

Kids playing atop the world's second longest river—Amazon River, Brazil

When the ground below is dry, stilts allow air to circulate and make it harder for animals and reptiles to enter. When the river rises 30-40 feet, stilts help keep this house dry. People here fish daily, gather rubber from rubber trees, and grow yucca, plantain, sugar cane and papaya. They rarely hunt. Animals have too many hiding places deep in the jungle.

Borneo,
Indonesia—
Southeast Asia

Brazil,
South America

Wood stilts 33 feet (10 m) high still don't guarantee a dry house—Selimbau, Borneo

The nearby Kapuas River rises so high during the rainy season that the first floor of this house has been flooded. Behind the canoes is a houseboat used to sleep and cook on while traveling down long rivers. Walking through this neighborhood with dry ground below is like walking through a forest. Look up and see house bottoms rather than leaves...a bit eerie, especially in the dark.

Batak Houses

Sumatra, Indonesia

Climb up a ladder to reach the front door. Remember to duck because the walls are so short! Once inside, there's more than enough room. Roofs are thatched steep and topped off with gables. Imagine the talent to weave the bamboo and build this large house without one single nail. In a land full of wildlife, from elephants to rhinos, a buffalo's horns are put on the top.

Drying rice outside a traditional Batak house —highlands surrounding Lake Toba, Sumatra

Most Batak people are farmers. They raise rice and enjoy it at breakfast, lunch and dinner! Roughly 10 houses face each other in a village. A broad central avenue travels down the middle, and is used to dry rice and catch up with friends. Water buffalo are special to Bataks. Some believe mounting their horns atop houses will keep harm away.

Sumatra, Indonesia—
Southeast Asia

Getting inside is like climbing up bunkbeds—highlands surrounding Lake Toba, Sumatra

Traditional house styles vary throughout Sumatra, but most are rectangular and built atop pile foundations. Walls are short and roofs are high and pointed. Space under the floor serves as running ground for pigs, chickens and small children, as well as storage for firewood and tools. The baskets hanging from floor level are little chicken houses.

Manyattas

Kenya & Tanzania

Sit or sleep, but watch your head if you stand! Walking inside houses is not popular here. Women take charge of the housing construction, weaving sticks in and out and adding some dung. The men build a fence made of prickly thornbushes, to encircle the houses and keep danger out. Grab a short stool. Cool off in the shade. But keep an eye towards the cattle munching grass on the plains.

Maasai outside their *manyatta* (house) and inside their *enyang'* (village)—Tanzania

Traditional Maasai and Samburu people move from place to place in search of fresh grass for their cattle. They survive using the leather, milk, blood and meat of their herds. The prickly fence surrounding the village protects the Maasai and their cattle at night from predators like hyenas. Zebras, elephants, and lions also share these vast grasslands called savannas. Lubegas are the traditional dress for the Maasai— long cotton cloths, usually red, brown or orange.

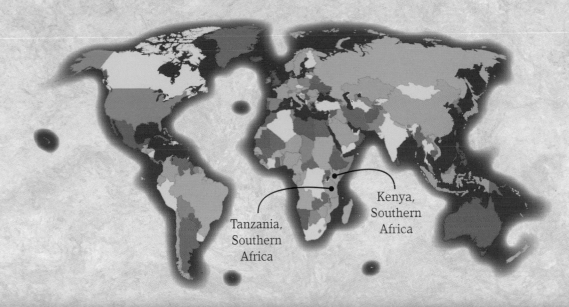

Tanzania, Southern Africa

Kenya, Southern Africa

A Samburu girl standing almost as tall as her house—Kenya

Houses are built as high as needed...about shoulder-height. They are covered in leaves, mud and cow dung. Dung is odorless once dry and repels rain better than clay. Women and girls keep their heads shaved. They also wear colorful bead necklaces...sometimes so many that you can't see their necks.

Painted Houses

Egypt

Colorful mud houses add pizzazz to the scene in a land of brown sand, pyramids and camels. A trip full of memories could be stored in an album. But here they are painted on the front of a house! The families of Luxor along the Nile River often share their adventures where others can see them. Find drawings of buildings, a boat or a bus. The words are in Arabic—so start right and read left.

Kicking up dust in a neighborhood game of soccer—Luxor, Egypt

Soccer (called football) is unquestionably the #1 sport and is played just about everywhere. Athletic fashion varies from traditional robes called *galabeas* to T-shirts and shorts. Once the game is over, galabeas win out for appropriate dress in this region. The Nile River flows 4,132 miles and is the longest river in the world. People living here find it essential for farming, fishing, transportation and tourism.

Egypt,
Northern Africa

Peeking out the window of her scrapbook-like house—Luxor, Egypt

Wooden shutters, not glass, cover small windows to keep out the sand.
Egyptians read and write in Arabic. Words and pictures are typically painted
on these houses after families make a journey important to their religion.

Tent Houses
Northern Africa and The Middle East

Nomads live in them. Camels carry them. They are sewn with goat hair and pitched in the sand. Tents make fine houses for those on the go, since they're a snap to put up and a snap to take down. With sheep, goats and camels as traveling companions, these nomads keep moving in search of fresh grass. At night the sky darkens and feet get a rest. Drift off to a folktale under a canopy of stars.

Herds of sheep and goats outside a cluster of Bedouin tents—Judean Desert, Israel

Bedouin houses are generally woven of black goatskins and called "black tents." Thanks to strong camels, they can be carried long distances. Bedouins live throughout the Middle East and live off camel, goat and sheep herding. They are experts at finding food and water, and tracking people and animals by the appearance of sand. Known as welcoming hosts, Bedouins make room for both invited and uninvited guests.

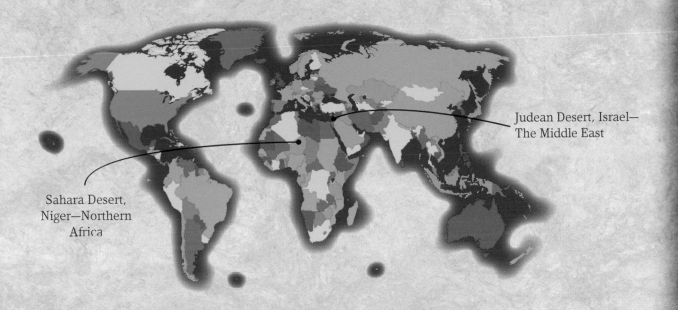

Judean Desert, Israel—
The Middle East

Sahara Desert,
Niger—Northern
Africa

Tuareg girls giggling outside their house—Sahara Desert, Niger

Tuaregs herd camels across the Sahara Desert in Niger. For fun, some race their camels in town. They are superb silversmiths who design crosses and charms thought to protect those who wear them. Tent roofs are typically made of 30-40 sheep or goatskins, tanned and sewn together.

Round Houses— Rondavels

South America and Africa

From high in the mountains to low on the grasslands, circles beat squares as the house shape of choice. Cold, rugged places can be chock full of rocks. Grasses and mud are used where it's warm. Look on the ground to see what's around. There are pluses to building with materials nearby. Boards limit shape, but clay and stones don't. Shingles cost money, but grass grows for free.

A Quero Indian boy outside his round stone house—Andes Mountains, Peru

The Quero Indians of Peru live and work at three levels of the Andes Mountains. This is the highest level. They raise sheep, llamas and alpacas since it is too cold to grow crops. The land is rugged and almost all travel is by horseback. Houses are built of stone, the only material around. Amazingly, they don't use mortar. They fit stones so tightly together that no spaces or gaps remain.

Peru—
South
America

Sudan—
Northern Africa

A young artist hard at work outside his house—southern Sudan

Circular houses in many parts of Africa are built in clusters close to fields. Frames are built using natural materials, such as: mud, clay, cow dung, grass, wood, sticks, or a mix. Roofs are usually thatched with bundles of grass or reeds, spread out in layers.

My House

Place a drawing or photo of your house above. Be an author and write your own description below.

If you've picked this book up from a library, good for you!
You can still complete this page by grabbing an adult to help
you make a photocopy. Take it home and enjoy!

Creative Team

Thank you to the brilliant photographers, illustrators and designers who brought this book to life!

Victor Englebert dreamed of being an explorer as a kid in Belgium. Through photography, writing and extreme guts, the dream became reality. He's traveled to the world's wild places in search of indigenous peoples and has documented the experiences in umpteen books and magazines, including 17 of his own.

David Farr took his first printing and photography classes in eighth grade. He loved both subjects—even the smelly printing inks and photo chemicals. In more than 25 years of work, he has designed hundreds of books and made photographs for himself, his family, and publications. His work includes art direction and design for *The Family Handyman,* a national home-improvement magazine.

Matt Kania loves maps and, as a kid, dreamed of making them. In school he studied geography and cartography and today makes maps for a living. Matt's favorite part about drawing maps is studying the places they represent. Many of the maps he creates can be found in books, magazines, videos, websites, and in public places like museums and schools.

Amy Learn, a Minneapolis College of Art and Design grad, grew up in a 100-year-old Iowa farmhouse like the one she illustrated for this book. As a kid, she pondered, "Will I be a cartoonist or a zookeeper?" Cartoonist won! She plans to bring her pictures to life in the world of animation.

Matt Mills, a Minneapolis College of Art and Design grad, hails from Kansas City, MO. Some of his family builds and some of his family draws. Matt can do both! So after hours of house illustration for this book, he's planning to design and build his own house to enjoy with his wife and a big slobbery dog.

VICTOR DAVID RICHARD

MATT K. ANGELA JAN

AMY SEAN STEPHEN

MATT M. nik

Richard Nowitz has been traveling the world with camera in hand for over 25 years. He is often sent on special assignments as a photographer for *National Geographic Kids* magazine. He has added magic to countless magazines and books with his photos, including a number of Insight Travel Guides.

Jan Reynolds is an author, photographer and adventurer who just can't get far enough away from it all. Her favorite thing is to escape to an extreme environment and hang out with the locals to learn about their culture. Check out www.janreynolds.com to see if Jan is out bungee jumping with Tibetan monks.

Sean Sprague is a 55 year-old photojournalist who has been traveling the world since he was 18. He works primarily with agencies that provide aid to people around the world. With Sean's photos and words, these agencies can spread excitement about their projects. Through his work, he has traveled to over 100 countries!

Stephen Trimble started taking pictures as a kid and hasn't stopped. He is biology student turned park ranger, turned award-winning photographer and writer. He's published 18 books, and when not traveling, writes from the attic of his 1915 house, built atop a hill at the base of the Rocky Mountains in Salt Lake City.

Nik Wheeler dreamed of being a professional soccer and cricket player as a kid. Little did he know he'd become a well-known photographer with travels to more than 100 countries. He and his family live in a wood California house, and visit their 600-year-old stone house in France. Its walls are over three feet thick!

Thank you to family and friends for your long show of support and enthusiasm.

And to The Loft Literary Center, Minneapolis College of Art and Design, Kristen Maija Peterson, my reviewers, my editor, and the many others I've met as a result of this project…for their education, insights and encouragement.

Think About It!
Discussion Questions

✱ How would you define the word "house"? What do you think is essential for any house?

✱ Which house in this book do you like best? Why?

✱ What materials are used to build these houses? Why?

✱ Who built the houses in this book? Who built your house? If your family had to build your own house, would it be different?

✱ Describe a climate different from your own. What styles of houses might be built there?

✱ Where has your family (parents/grandparents/great-grandparents/and beyond) lived? What did/do their houses look like?

✱ Three different house styles come from one country in this book. What country is it?

✱ Compare and contrast living in the city versus living in the country. How are house styles similar and different?

✱ What would you imagine the insides of these houses to look like...the kitchen, bedrooms, furniture, etc.?

✱ How does the land surrounding these houses compare with the land outside of yours? Is there a grass yard? Sidewalks?

✱ What different factors determine the style of house someone lives in?

Do It!
Activity Ideas

✔ Find the dictionary definition of "house." Write your own definition.

✔ Draw the house you live in.

✔ Take photographs of the house you live in and of other houses in your community.

✔ Compare and contrast your house with a house in the book. Create two columns with the headings: **Similar** and **Different**. Create a list under each, thinking of everything you can such as: building materials, decoration, families, environment, culture, and what the house sits on.

✔ Create a timeline for the houses you have lived in. Include location, dates, photos and/or drawings, and your comments.

✔ Many of the houses in this book are built according to tradition. Generally, these skills are passed down from generation to generation. Discover a special skill of a parent, grandparent, or someone else close to you. Have that person teach you the skill and keep it a tradition!

✔ Pick out one house from the book. Come up with 10 questions about the house and see if you can locate the answers using other resources.

✔ Pick out a house style not featured in this book. Do your own research and report on it.

✔ Build a model house of your choice with readily available materials (i.e., mud, sticks, ice, popsicle sticks, cotton, etc.). Be creative!

✔ If you lived in Luxor, Egypt how would you paint the front of your house?

✔ Review the "Creative Team" on page 31. Do any of their careers seem interesting to you? What kind of work would you like to do in the future?

Check 'Em Out!

Due to space, only a few of the unique house styles around the world fit into this book. Here are several more you might want to look into...

1. Alpine houses—Switzerland
2. Arctic homes raised above the ground—Canada and Greenland
3. Barrel-vaulted houses—Thira, Greece
4. Caribbean painted timber houses
5. Cave houses—Gaudix, Spain and central Tunisia
6. Cottages with thatched roofs—England
7. Dogon villages—Mali
8. Clay huts—Cameroon
9. High-rise apartment buildings—large cities around the world
10. Painted adobe houses—Navrongo, Ghana
11. Log houses—Siberia, Canada and northern regions
12. Monasteries & temples where monks live and worship—mostly Asia
13. Open-sided houses—South Pacific
14. Ndebele painted houses—South Africa
15. Screen houses—Japan
16. Siberian tents made in summer from birch tree bark—Russia
17. Treehouses—Indonesia and Papua New Guinea
18. Trulli houses—Apulia, Italy
19. Tufa-cone houses—Cappadocia, Turkey
20. Gers and yurts—Mongolia and Kazakhstan (Central Asia)